GENERATIONS

BABY BOOMERS 1950–1963

Take the 3,548,000 babies born in 1950. Bundle them into a batch, bounce them all over the bountiful land that is America. What do you get? Boom. The biggest, boomiest boom ever known in history.

—Sylvia Porter
New York Post (May 4, 1951)

Produced by
Alfred Music Publishing Co., Inc.
P.O. Box 10003
Van Nuys, CA 91410-0003
alfred.com

Printed in USA.

ISBN-10: 0-7390-6554-8

ISBN-13: 978-0-7390-6554-9

Cover Photos:
© istockphoto/anzeletti, biffspandex, eliadric, GeofferyHolman, hundreddays, Imagesbybarbara, ParentesiGrafica, schlot
© stock.xchng/andrewatla, deebeee999, lxine, suzula, mattosense

FOREWORD

The term "baby boomers" immediately brings to mind a mix of significant events and issues: the Civil Rights Movement, the assassination of President John Fitzgerald Kennedy, the Vietnam War, the birth of "suburbia," Woodstock, feminism, free love, and more. The baby boom generation witnessed, and initiated, some of the pivotal moments in American history.

After World War II ended in 1945, thousands of soldiers returned home to the United States ready to begin their adult lives. Bolstered by a strong economy and the far-reaching GI Bill, which made homes affordable, young couples saw a chance to live the American Dream, which had been shadowed by the Great Depression and the war. Starting a family was central to this dream. In stark contrast to the low birth rates during the war, from 1946 to 1964 the country experienced the highest birth rates and fastest population growth ever. At the end of the boom, almost half of the population was under the age of 25. From the cities to the newly formed suburbs, the baby boomers were destined to change America—through sheer size alone.

Music was prominent during this change, becoming central to the generation. Their favorite songs—"bubblegum" pop, rock and roll, and even protest songs—can be found in the two volumes of *Generations: Baby Boomers.* The first volume explores hits from 1950 to 1963, the music that boomers heard during childhood. These songs both shaped their early years and became the basis for their later rebellions. This music captures the innocent style of the 1950s, such as the catchy and squeaky-clean songs *All I Have to Do Is Dream* (The Everly Brothers) and *Only You (And You Alone)* (The Platters). There are songs in the "doo-wop" style, which featured tight vocal harmonies and nonsense syllables, such as the hits *A Teenager In Love* (Dion and the Belmonts) and *Blue Moon* (The Marcels). There are also timeless standards, such as *It Was a Very Good Year* and *Mack the Knife,* which were made famous by the crooners Frank Sinatra and Bobby Darin, respectively. There are also the first inklings of popular music becoming a lightning rod for action and experimentation. Bob Dylan revolted against war in *Blowin' in the Wind,* in which he asked a series of questions about the nature of man in the modern world. *Puff (The Magic Dragon)* became a theme song for recreational drug use, despite author Peter Yarrow's adamant denial that the song had any such connotations.

The baby boomer generation is unique in American history; it is doubtful that such a sudden and protracted population increase will happen again. This collection is designed to spark nostalgic memories for those who grew up during that time. For new players, it is an introduction to this great music. Enjoy discovering or revisiting this important time in the history of popular music, the music of the *Baby Boomers!*

Each piece in this collection has been carefully arranged for late elementary to early intermediate pianists. Lyrics are included as well as suggestions for fingering, pedaling, and phrasing.

TABLE OF CONTENTS

All I Have to Do Is Dream

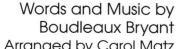

Words and Music by
Boudleaux Bryant
Arranged by Carol Matz

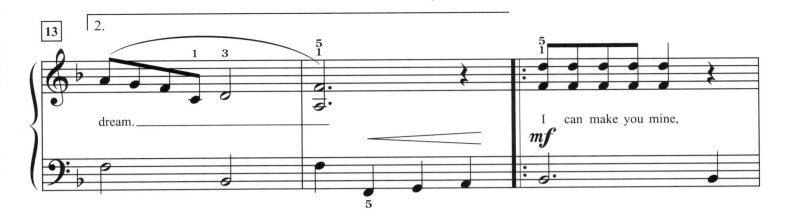

dream.

I can make you mine,

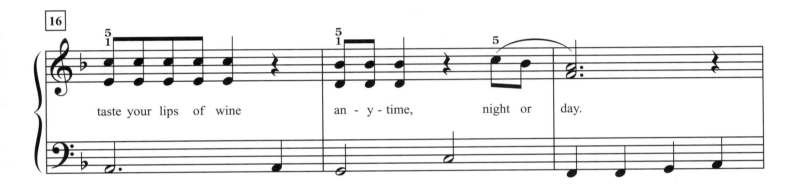

taste your lips of wine an-y-time, night or day.

On-ly trou-ble is, gee whiz, I'm dream-in' my life a-

way. I need you so, that I could die. I

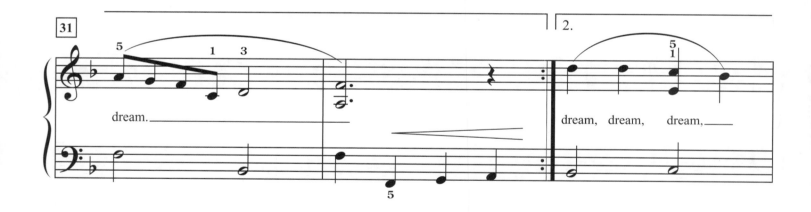

Blowin' in the Wind

Words and Music by Bob Dylan
Arranged by Carol Matz

Blue Moon

Music by Richard Rodgers
Lyrics by Lorenz Hart
Arranged by Carol Matz

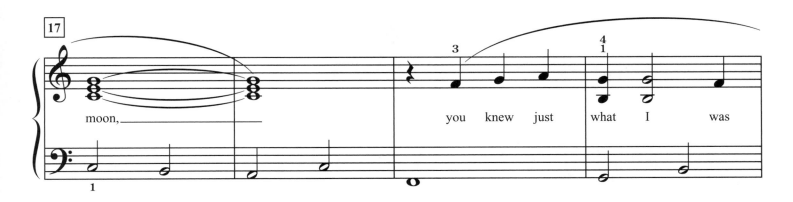

moon, _____ you knew just what I was

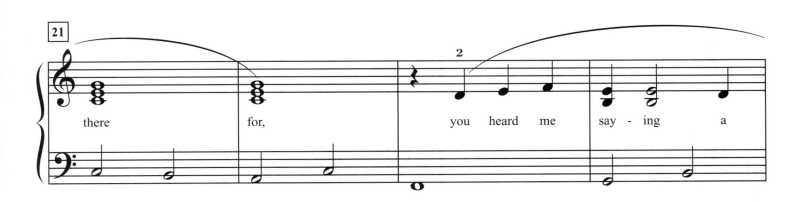

there for, you heard me say - ing a

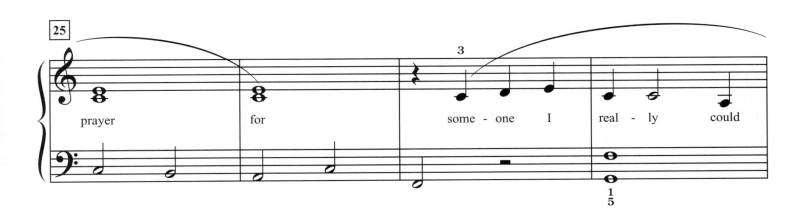

prayer for some - one I real - ly could

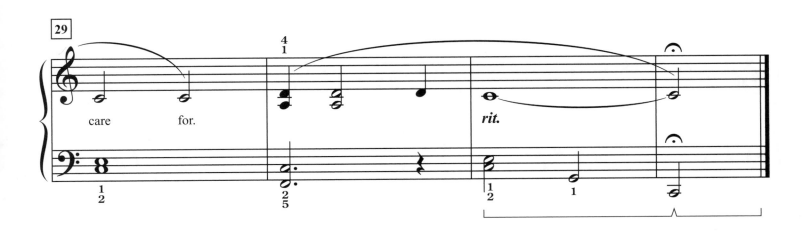

care for. *rit.*

Bye Bye Love

Words and Music by
Boudleaux Bryant and Felice Bryant
Arranged by Carol Matz

hel - lo   emp - ti - ness;___   I feel like I could die.___

___   Bye bye, my love,___ good - bye.___

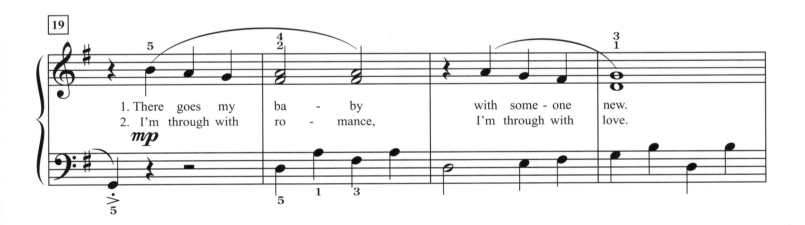

1. There goes my   ba - by   with some - one   new.
2. I'm through with   ro - mance,   I'm through with   love.

mp

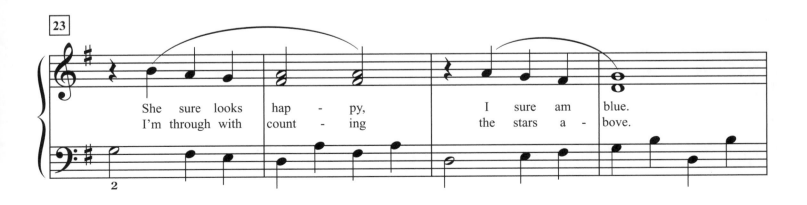

She sure looks   hap - py,   I   sure am   blue.
I'm through with   count - ing   the stars a - bove.

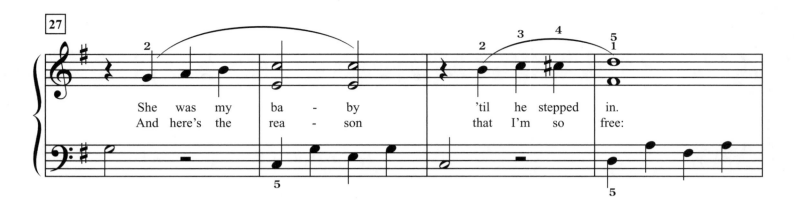

She was my ba - by 'til he stepped in.
And here's the rea - son that I'm so free:

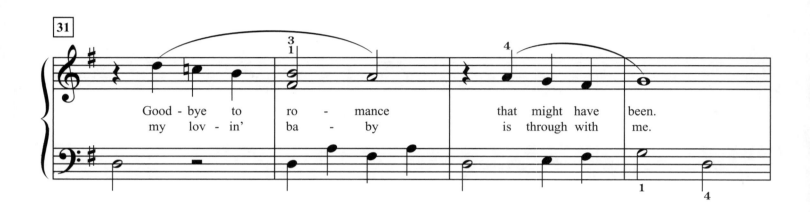

Good - bye to ro - mance that might have been.
my lov - in' ba - by is through with me.

Bye bye love,____ bye bye

mf

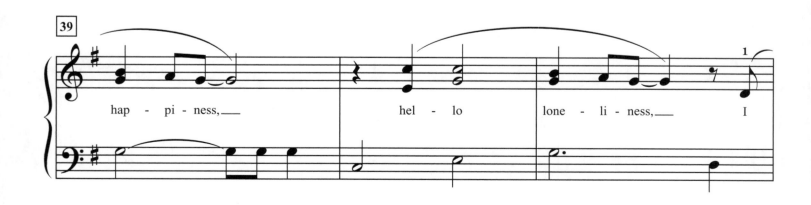

hap - pi - ness,____ hel - lo lone - li - ness,____ I

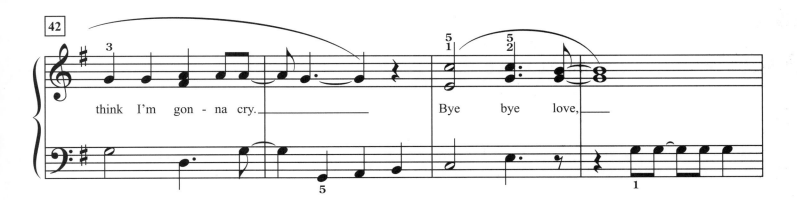

think I'm gon-na cry._____ Bye bye love,_____

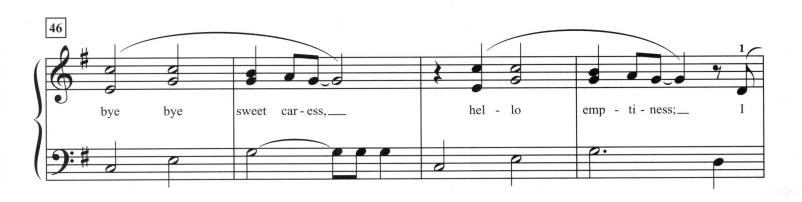

bye bye sweet car - ess,___ hel - lo emp - ti - ness;___ I

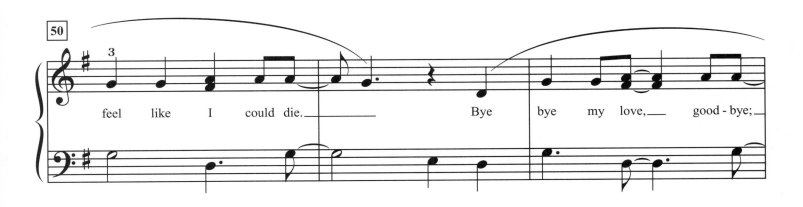

feel like I could die._____ Bye bye my love,___ good - bye;___

_____ good - bye, my love,___ good - bye.___

Great Balls of Fire

Words and Music by
Otis Blackwell and Jack Hammer
Arranged by Carol Matz

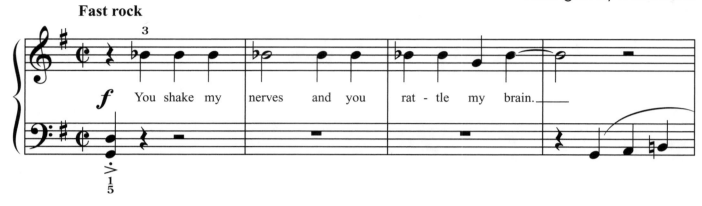

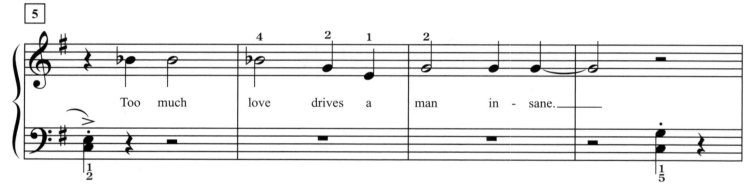

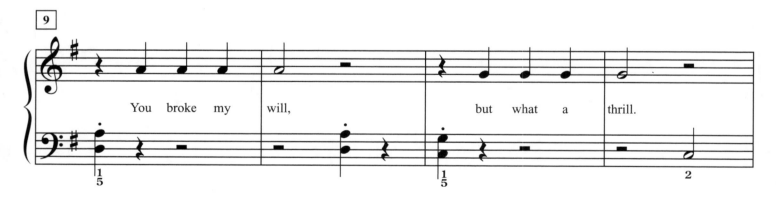

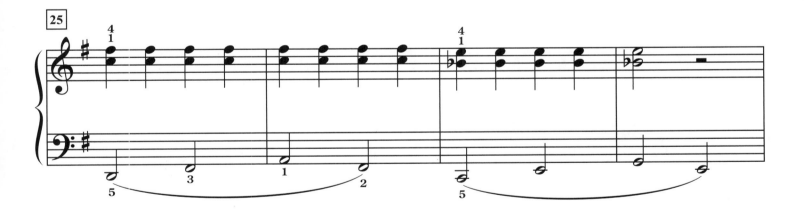

Good - ness gra - cious, great balls of fire!

Earth Angel

Words and Music by Jesse Belvin
Arranged by Carol Matz

love you for-ev - er_____ and ev-er more. I'm just a fool,_____

a fool in love with you.

fell for you, and I knew the vi - sion of your love's love-li -

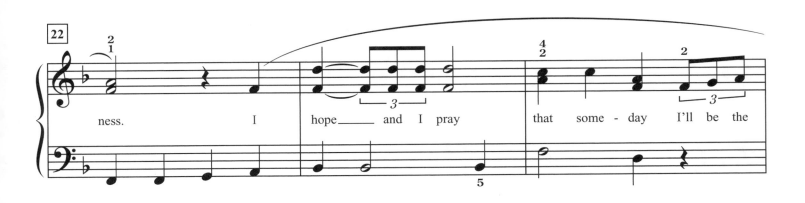

ness. I hope_____ and I pray that some - day I'll be the

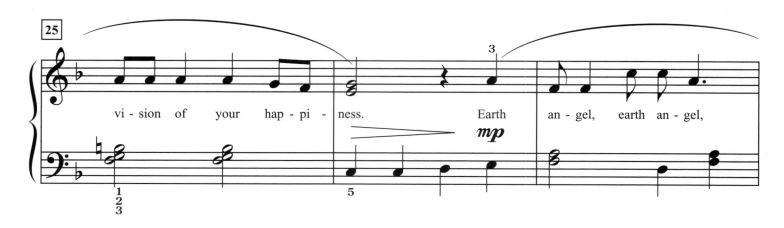

vi - sion of your hap - pi - ness. Earth an - gel, earth an - gel,

please be___ mine, my dar - ling, dear,___ love you all the time.

I'm just a fool,___ a fool in love with you.

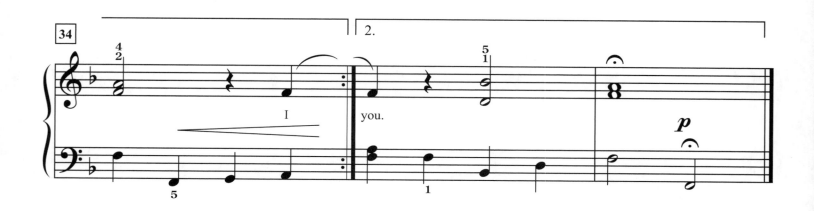

I you.

I'm Walkin'

Words and Music by
Antoine Domino and Dave Bartholomew
Arranged by Carol Matz

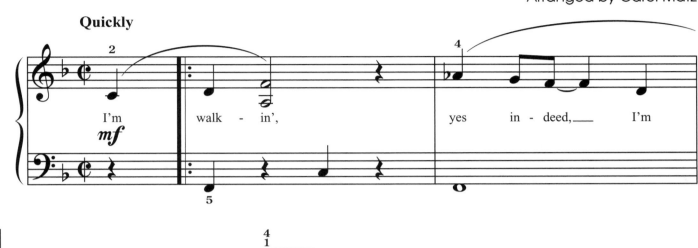

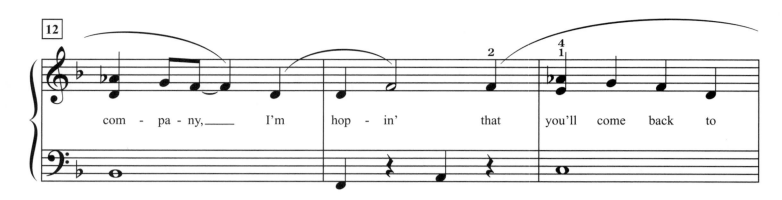

12 com - pa - ny,_____ I'm hop - in' that you'll come back to

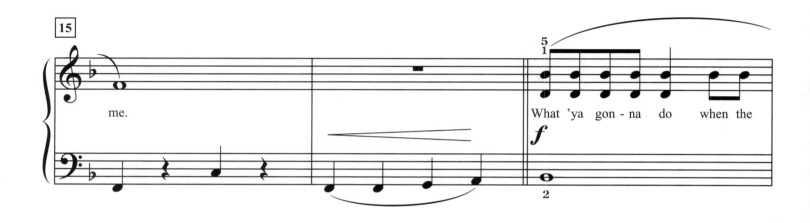

15 me. What 'ya gon - na do when the

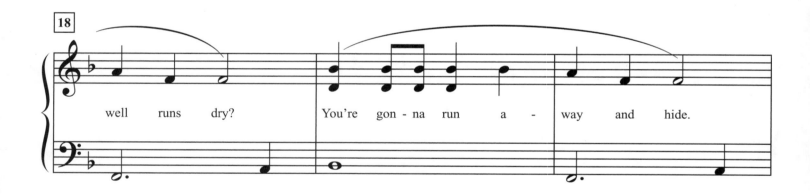

18 well runs dry? You're gon - na run a - way and hide.

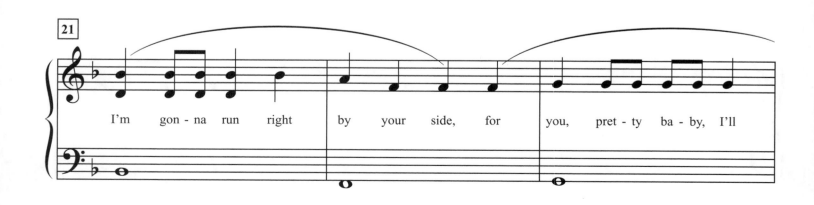

21 I'm gon - na run right by your side, for you, pret - ty ba - by, I'll

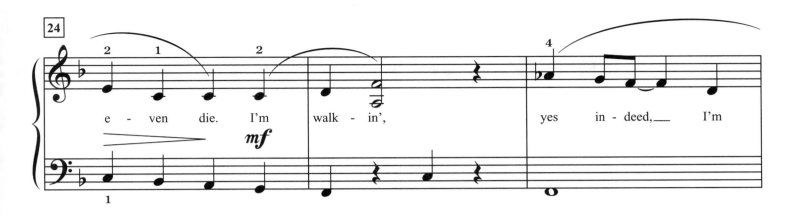

e - ven die. I'm walk - in', yes in - deed,___ I'm

talk - in' 'bout you and me,___ I'm hop - in' that

1.

you'll come back to me. I'm

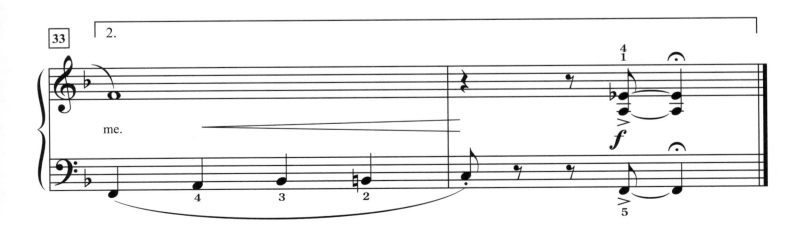

2.

me.

It Was a Very Good Year

Words and Music by Ervin Drake
Arranged by Carol Matz

Moderately slow, freely

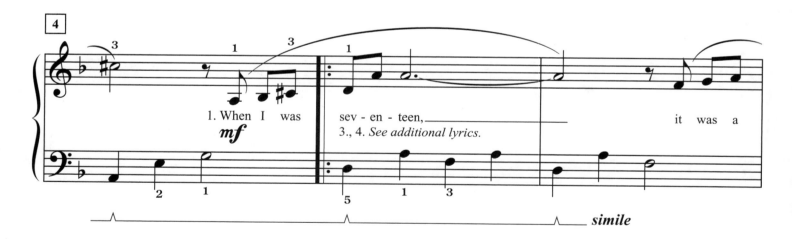

1. When I was sev - en - teen,_____ it was a
3., 4. *See additional lyrics.*

simile

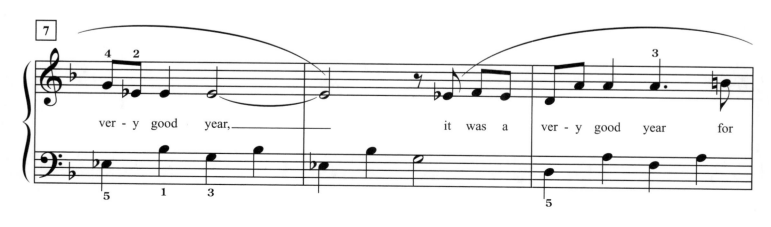

ver - y good year,_____ it was a ver - y good year for

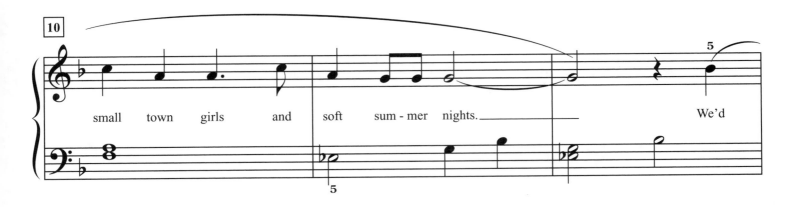

small town girls and soft sum-mer nights._____ We'd

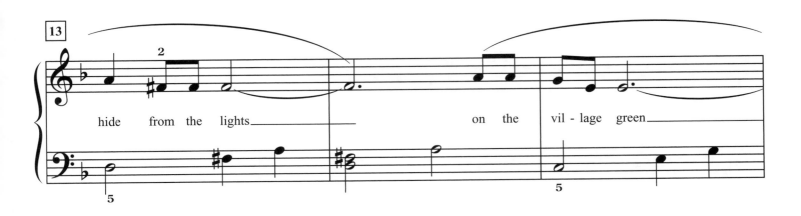

hide from the lights_____ on the vil-lage green_____

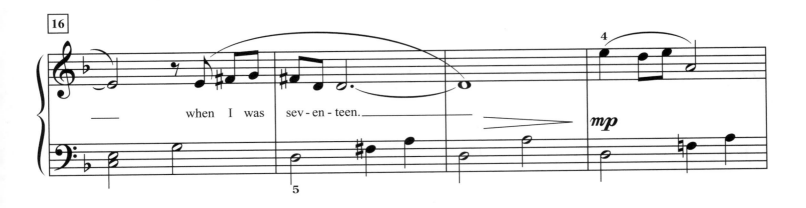

____ when I was sev-en-teen._____

2. When I was

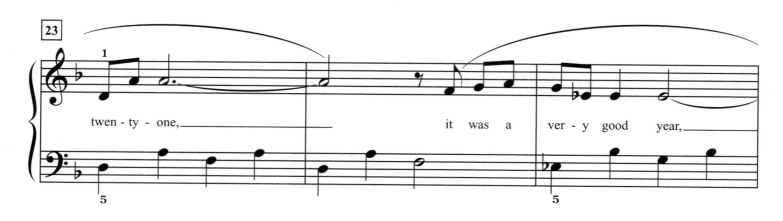

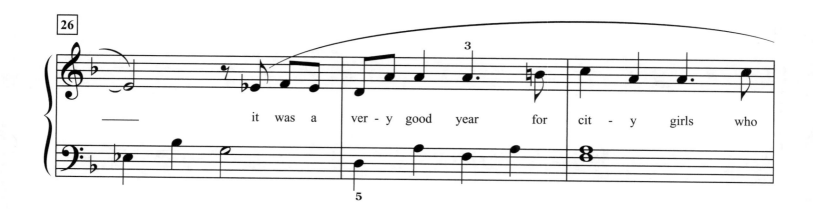

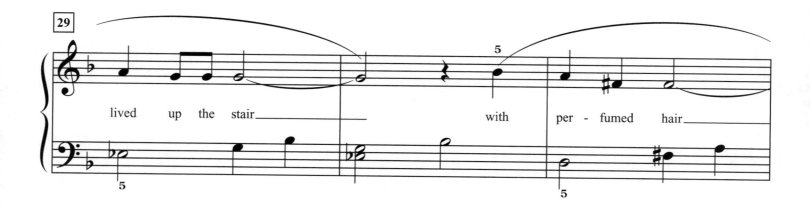

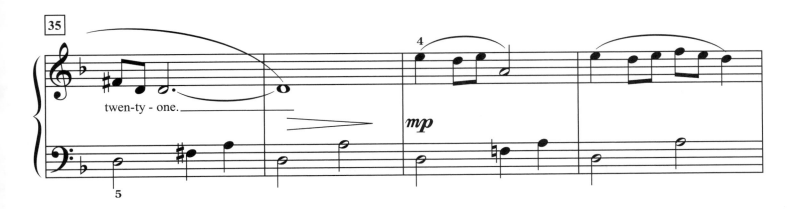

Verse 3:
When I was thirty-five, it was a very good year,
It was a very good year for blue-blooded girls of independent means.
We'd ride in limousines their chauffeurs would drive
When I was thirty-five.

Verse 4:
But now the days are short, I'm in the autumn of the year,
And now I think of my life as vintage wine from the old kegs.
From the brim to the dregs it poured sweet and clear;
It was a very good year.

It's My Party

Words and Music by
Herb Wiener, John Gluck and Wally Gold
Arranged by Carol Matz

It's my par - ty and I'll cry if I want to,

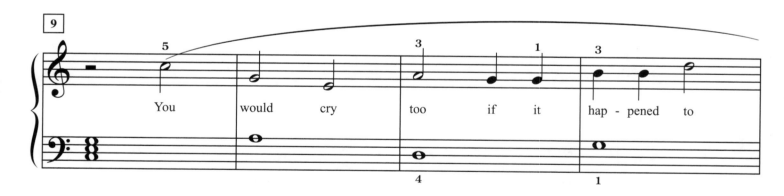

cry if I want to, cry if I want to.

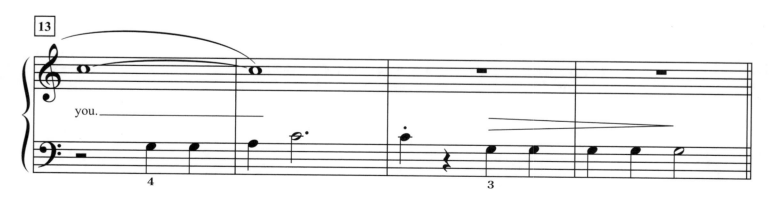

You would cry too if it hap - pened to you.

Itsy Bitsy Teenie Weenie Yellow Polka Dot Bikini

Words and Music by
Paul J. Vance and Lee Pockriss
Arranged by Carol Matz

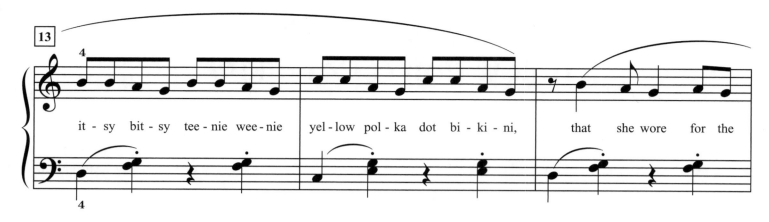

itsy bitsy teenie weenie yellow polka dot bikini, that she wore for the

first time today. An itsy bitsy teenie weenie yellow polka dot bikini,

so in the locker she wanted to stay. *(Two, three, four, stick around, we'll*

tell you more.) 2. She was a - wanted to stay.
3. Now she's a -

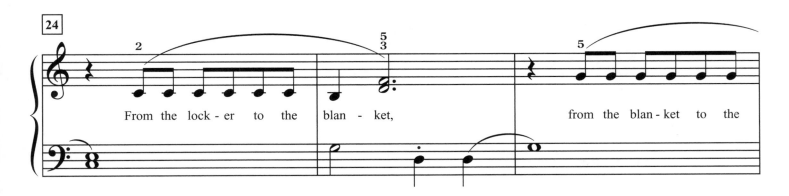

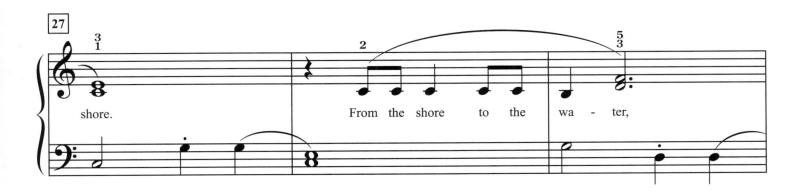

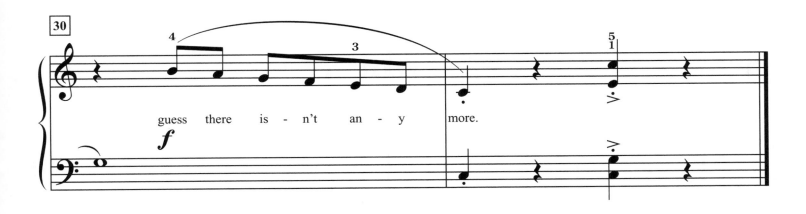

Verse 2:
She was afraid to come out in the open,
And so a blanket around her she wore.
She was afraid to come out in the open,
And so she sat bundled up on the shore.
(Two, three, four, tell the people what she wore.)

Verse 3:
Now she's afraid to come out of the water,
And I wonder what she's gonna do.
Now she's afraid to come out of the water,
And the poor little girl's turning blue.
(Two, three, four, tell the people what she wore.)

James Bond Theme

By Monty Norman
Arranged by Carol Matz

The Lion Sleeps Tonight

New Lyric and Revised Music by
George David Weiss, Hugo Peretti and Luigi Creatore
Arranged by Carol Matz

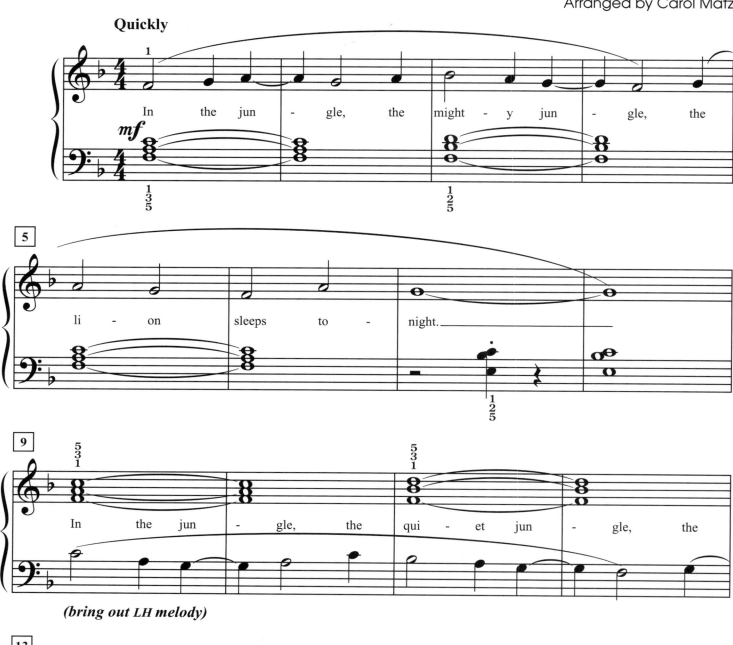

(bring out LH melody)

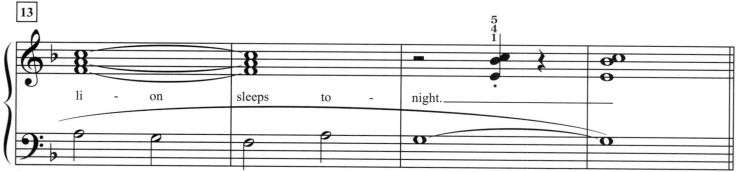

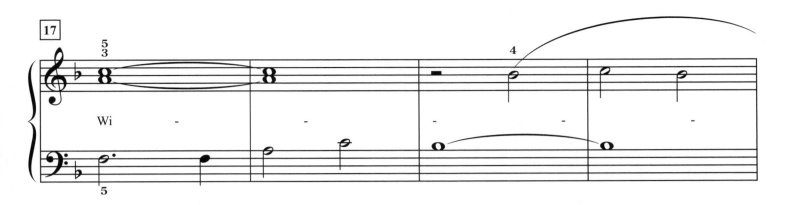

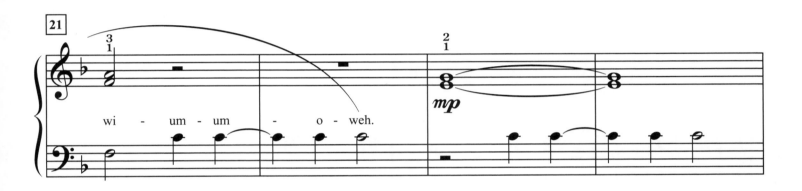

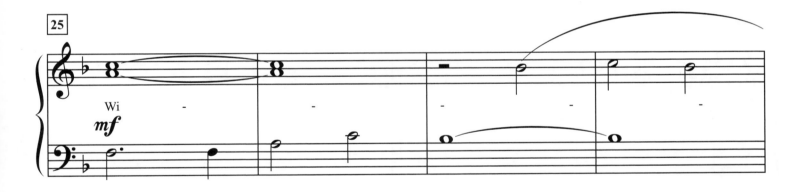

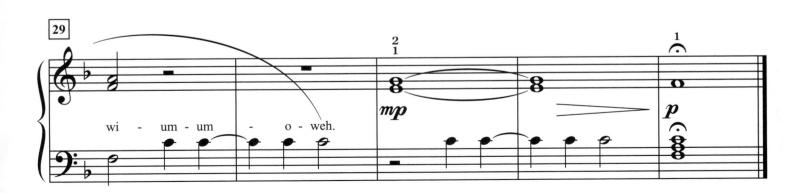

Mack the Knife

English Words By Marc Blitzstein
Original German Words By Bert Brecht
Music by Kurt Weill
Arranged by Carol Matz

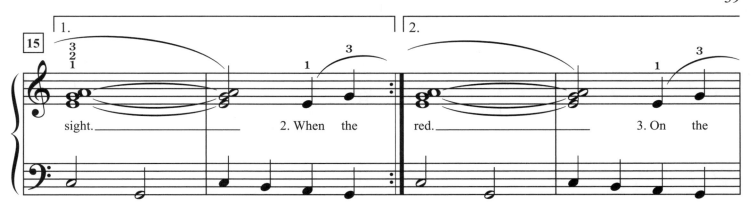

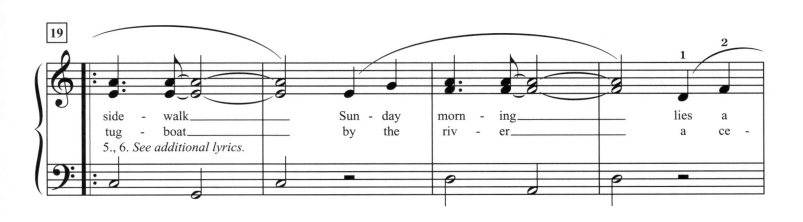

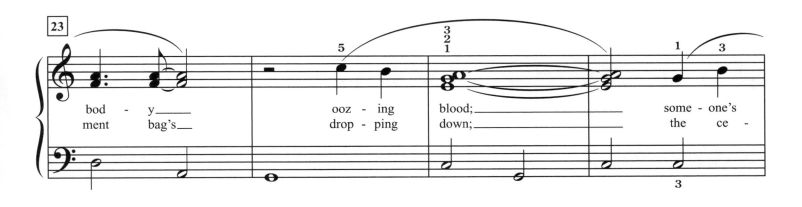

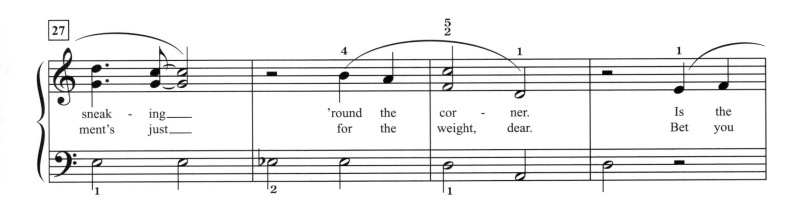

40

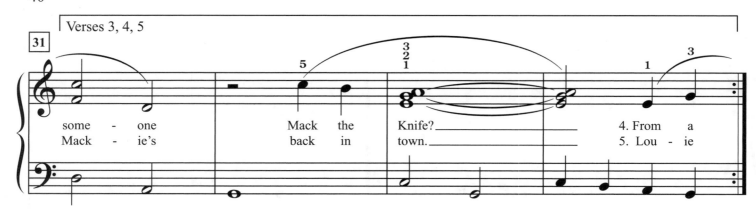

some - one   Mack the   Knife?_____   4. From a
Mack - ie's   back in   town._____   5. Lou - ie

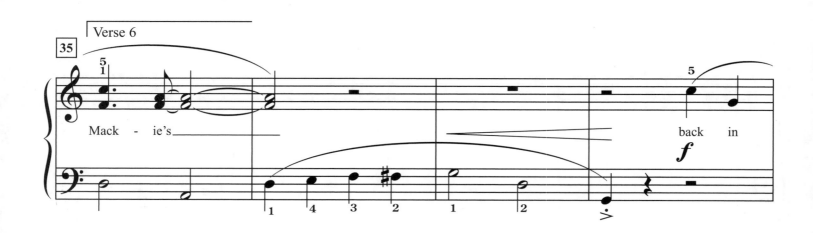

Mack - ie's_____   back in

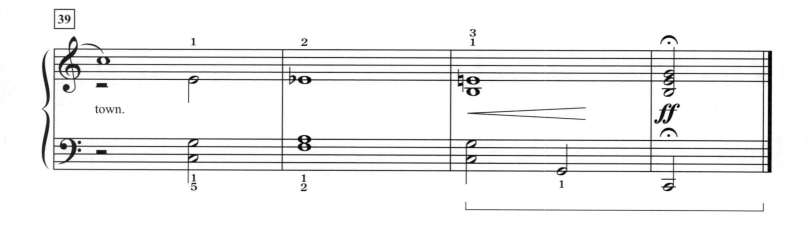

town.

Verse 5:
Louie Miller disappeared, dear,
After drawing out his cash;
And Macheath spends like a sailor.
Did our boy do something rash?

Verse 6:
Sukey Tawdry, Jenny Diver,
Polly Peachum, Lucy Brown.
Oh, the line forms on the right, dear,
Now that Mackie's back in town.

Misty

Words by Johnny Burke
Music by Erroll Garner
Arranged by Carol Matz

42

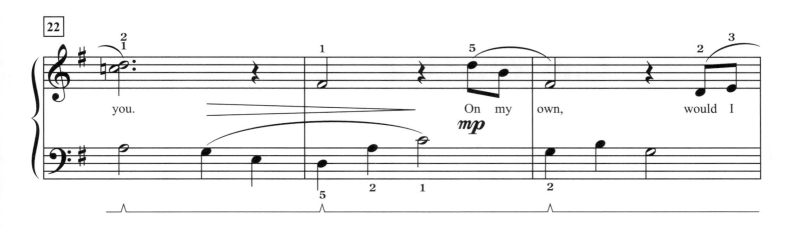

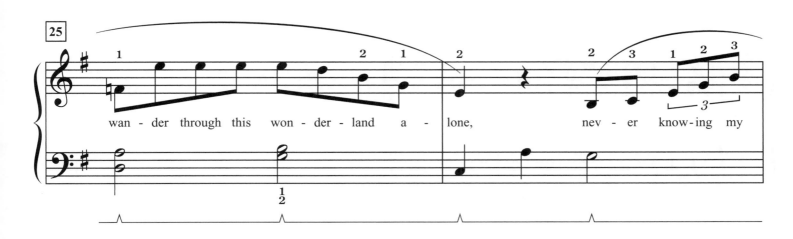

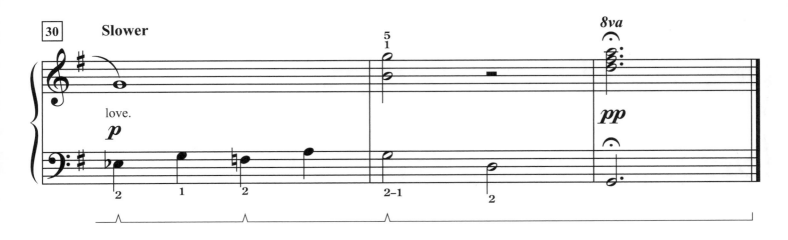

Only You (And You Alone)

Words and Music by
Buck Ram and Andre Rand
Arranged by Carol Matz

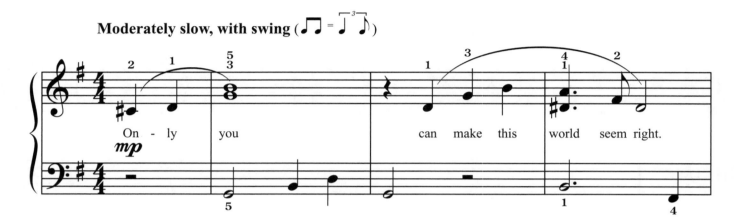

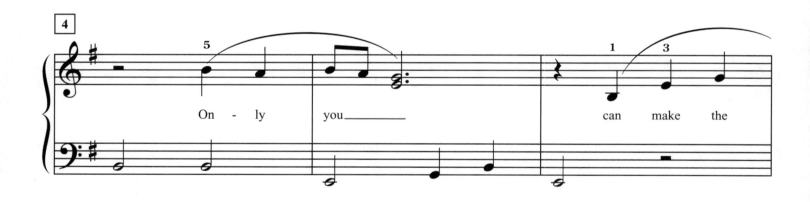

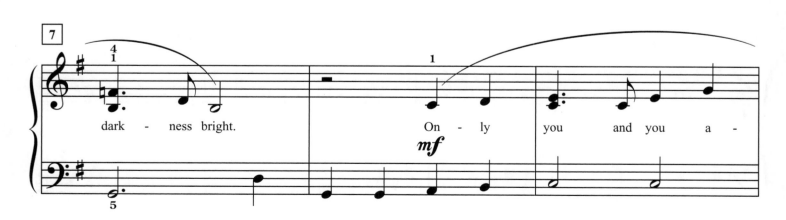

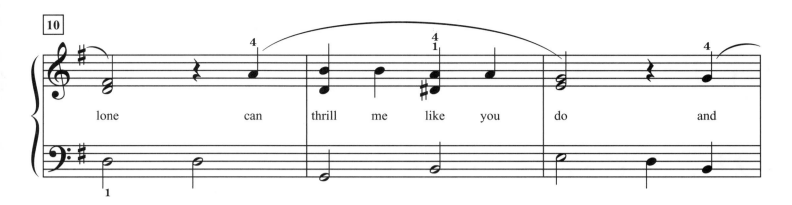

lone   can   thrill   me   like   you   do   and

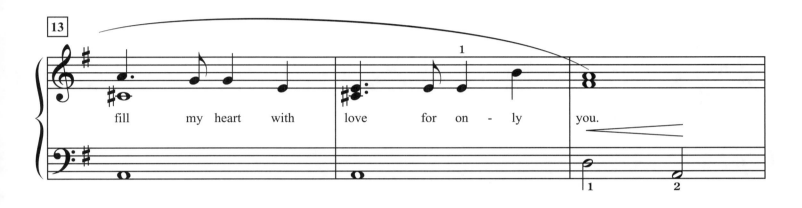

fill   my   heart   with   love   for   on   -   ly   you.

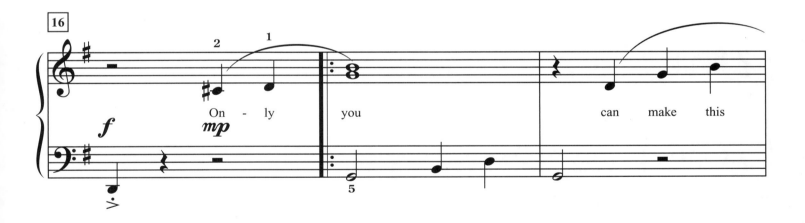

On - ly   you   can   make   this

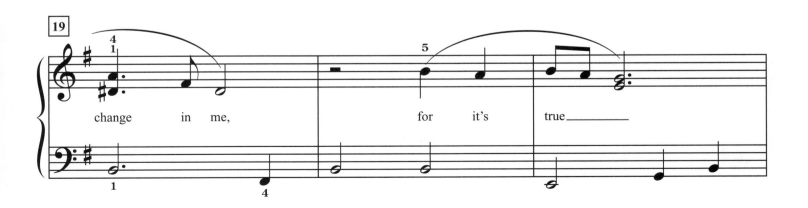

change   in   me,   for   it's   true_____

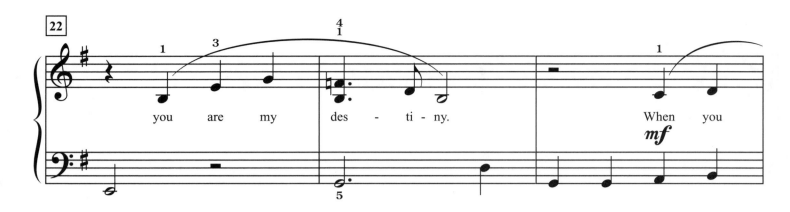

you are my des - ti - ny. When you

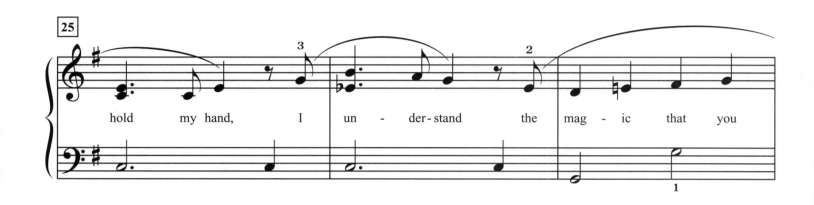

hold my hand, I un - der - stand the mag - ic that you

do. You're my dream come true, my one and on - ly

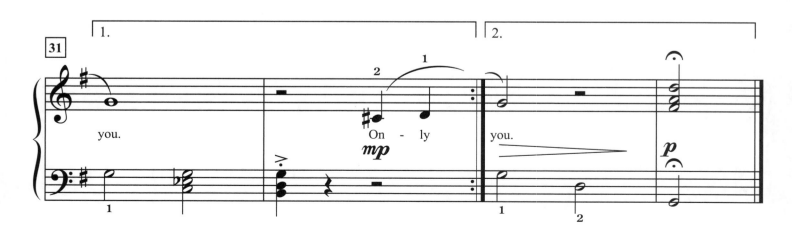

you. On - ly you.

Puff (The Magic Dragon)

Words and Music by
Peter Yarrow and Leonard Lipton
Arranged by Carol Matz

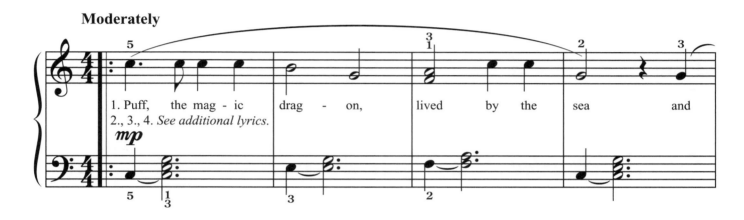

1. Puff, the mag - ic drag - on, lived by the sea and
2., 3., 4. *See additional lyrics.*

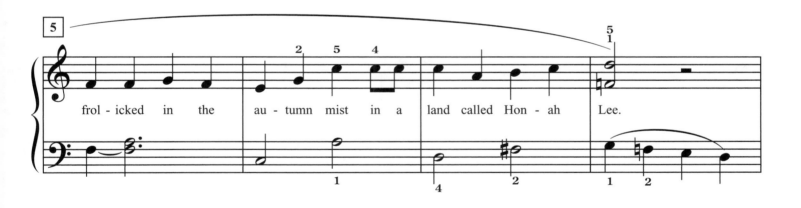

frol - icked in the au - tumn mist in a land called Hon - ah Lee.

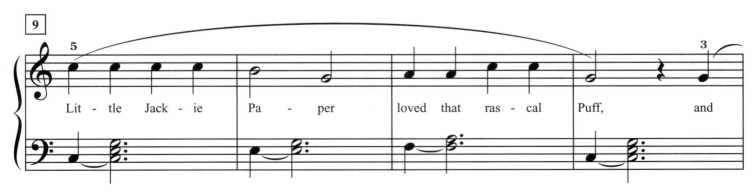

Lit - tle Jack - ie Pa - per loved that ras - cal Puff, and

48

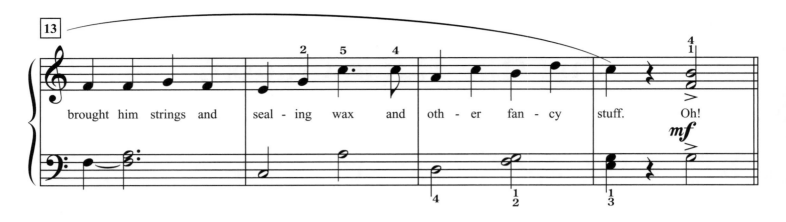

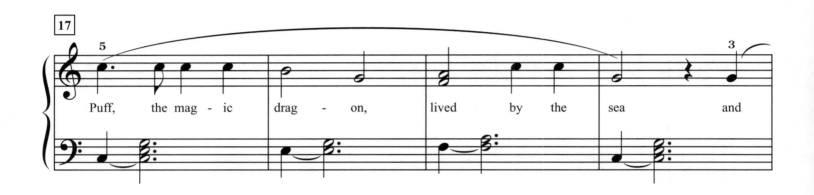

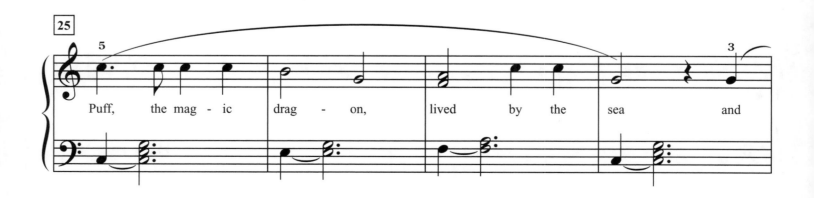

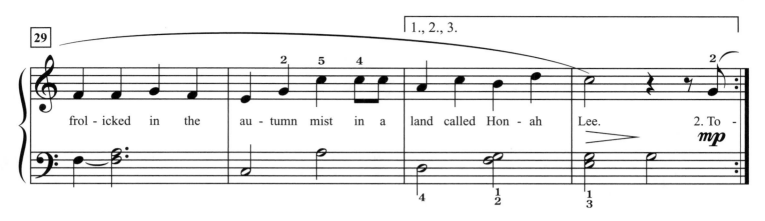

frol - icked in the au - tumn mist in a land called Hon - ah Lee. 2. To -

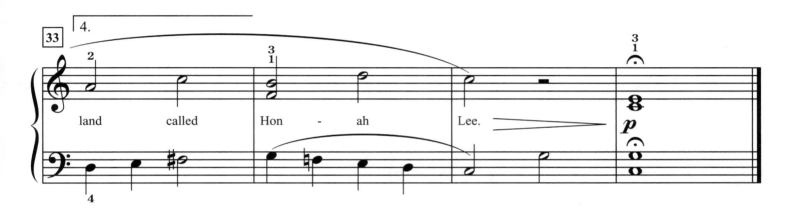

land called Hon - ah Lee.

Verse 2:
Together they would travel on a boat with billowed sail,
Jackie left a lookout perched on Puff's gigantic tail.
Noble kings and princes would bow when e'er they came.
Pirate ships would low'r their flag when Puff roared out his name. Oh!
(To Chorus)

Verse 3:
A dragon lives forever, but not so little boys;
Painted wings and giant rings make way for other toys.
One grey night it happened, Jackie Paper came no more.
And Puff, that mighty dragon, he ceased his fearless roar. Oh!
(To Chorus)

Verse 4:
His head was bent in sorrow, green scales fell like rain.
Puff no longer went to play along the cherry lane.
Without his life-long friend, Puff could not be brave,
So Puff, that mighty dragon, sadly slipped into his cave. Oh!
(To Chorus)

Runaround Sue

Words and Music by
Dion DiMucci and Ernest Maresca
Arranged by Carol Matz

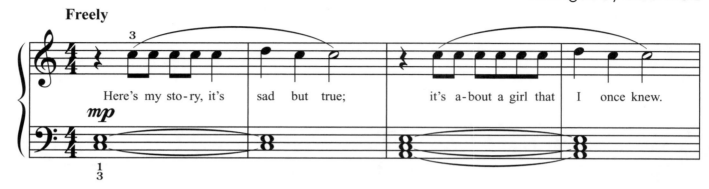

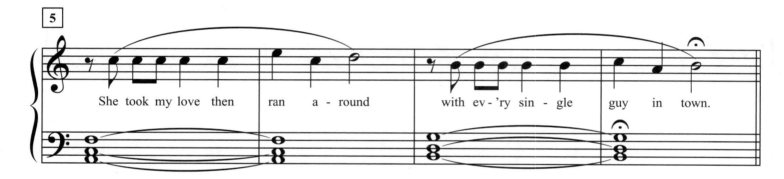

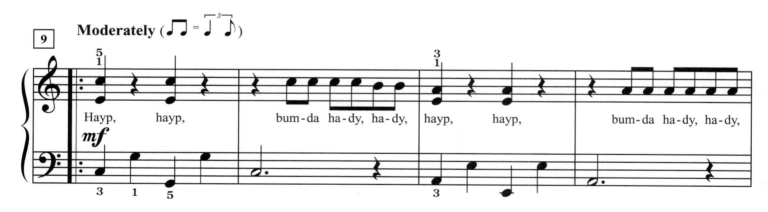

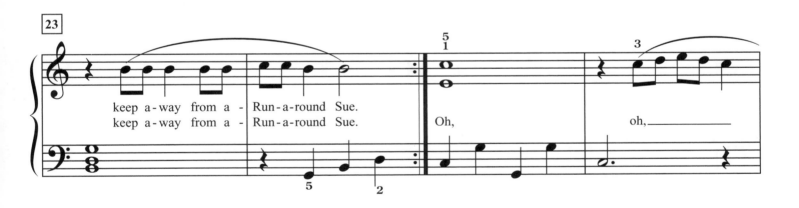

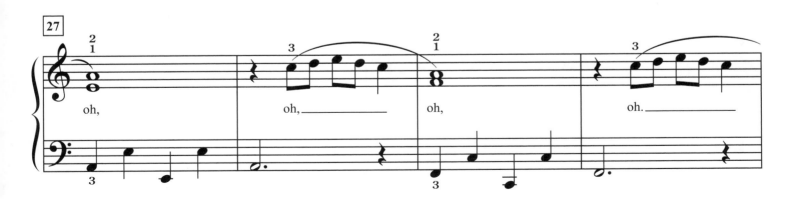

She likes to trav-el a-round,____ she'll

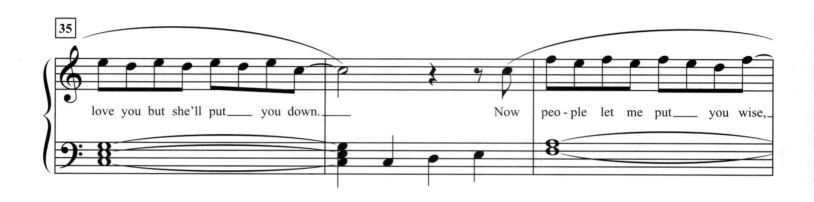

love you but she'll put____ you down.____ Now peo-ple let me put____ you wise,

Sue goes out with oth-er guys. Here's the

mor-al of the sto-ry from the guy who knows____ I fell in love and my

love still grows.__ Ask an - y fool that she ev - er knew,__ they'll say

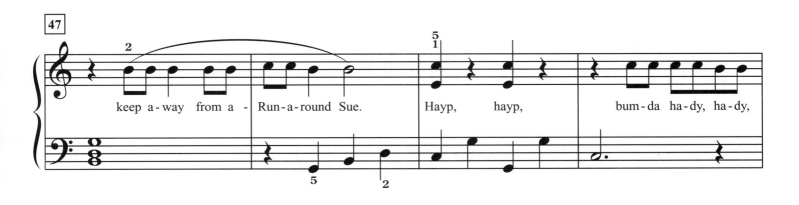

keep a - way from a - Run-a-round Sue. Hayp, hayp, bum - da ha - dy, ha - dy,

hayp, hayp, bum - da ha - dy, ha - dy, hayp, hayp,

bum - da ha - dy, ha - dy, hayp!

Runaway

Words and Music by
Del Shannon and Max Crook
Arranged by Carol Matz

Moderately fast

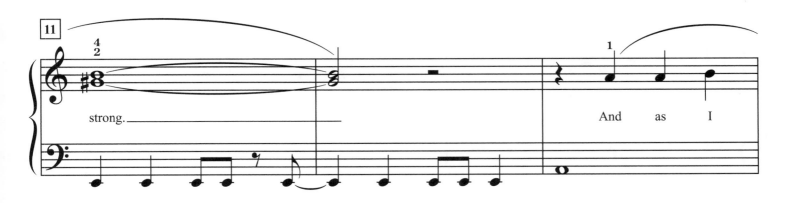

strong._____ And as I

still walk on___ I think of the things we've done___ to - geth - er a -

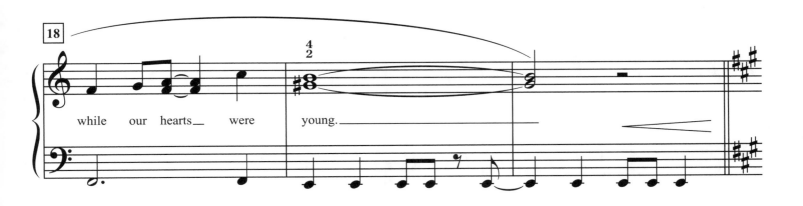

while our hearts___ were young._____

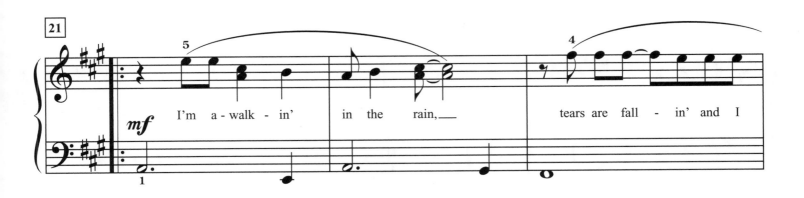

I'm a - walk - in' in the rain,___ tears are fall - in' and I

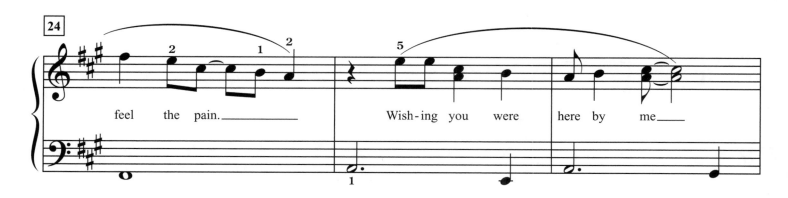

feel the pain._____ Wish-ing you were here by me____

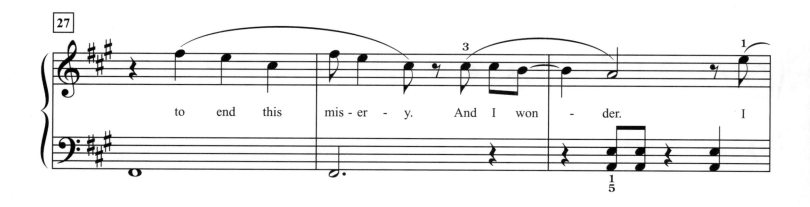

to end this mis - er - y. And I won - der. I

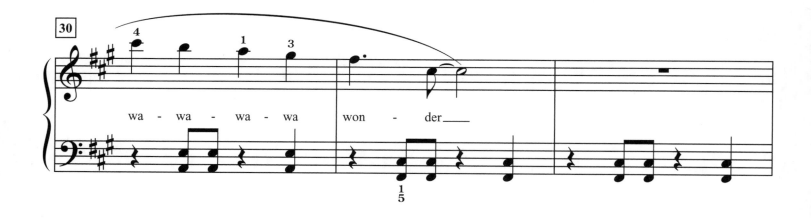

wa - wa - wa - wa won - der____

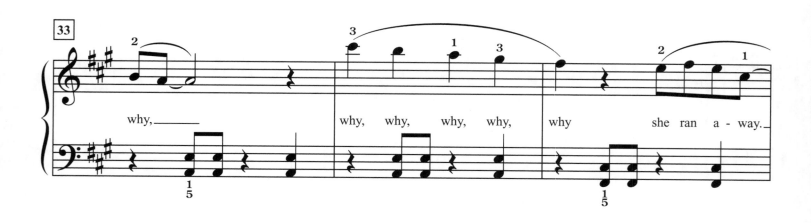

why,_____ why, why, why, why, why she ran a - way.

57

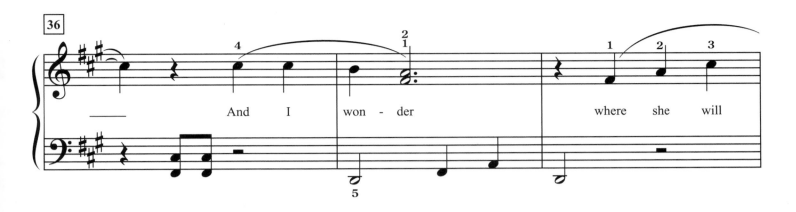

And I won - der where she will

stay,_____ my lit - tle run - a - way, a -

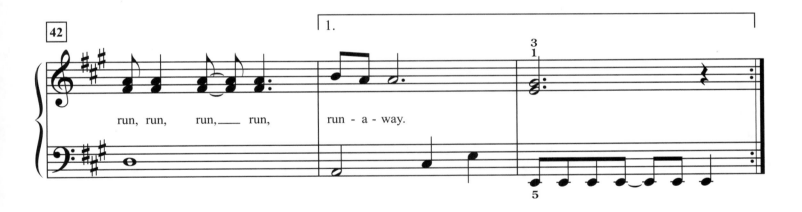

1.

run, run, run,___ run, run - a - way.

2.

run - a - way, a - run, run, run,___ run, run - a - way. *rit.*

Save the Last Dance for Me

Words by Doc Pomus
Music by Mort Shuman
Arranged by Carol Matz

get who's tak - ing you home and in whose arms you're gon - na be.____

mf

to Coda ✇

So dar - lin', save the last dance____ for

1.

me.

2. Oh, I

mp

2.

me.

Ba - by, don't you know I love you so?____ Can't you feel it when we

touch? I will nev - er, nev - er let you go.____

D.S. al Coda

I love you oh so much. 3. You can

mp

Coda

me. Oh, dar - lin', save the

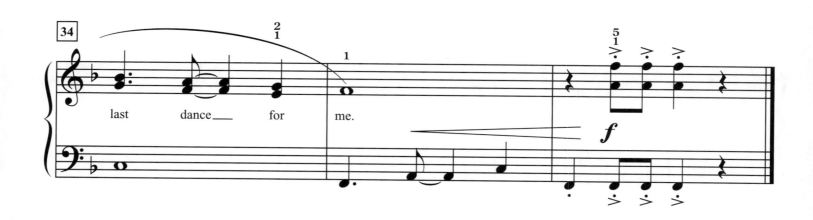

last dance____ for me.

f

Sixteen Candles

Words and Music by
Luther Dixon and Allyson Khent
Arranged by Carol Matz

for I'll be wish - ing____ that you love____ me

too. You're on - ly six - teen,

but you're my teen - age queen. You're the

pret - ti - est, love - li - est girl I've ev - er seen.

Sixteen can - dles____ in my heart will

glow for - ev - er and ev - er,____

for I love____ you so. You're on - ly six -

so. For I love you so.

Splish Splash

Words and Music by
Bobby Darin and Jean Murray
Arranged by Carol Matz

Moderately fast

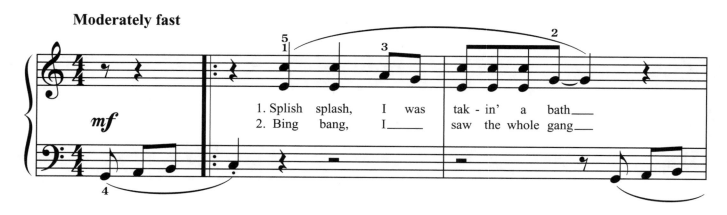

1. Splish splash, I was   tak - in' a bath___
2. Bing bang, I___ saw the whole gang___

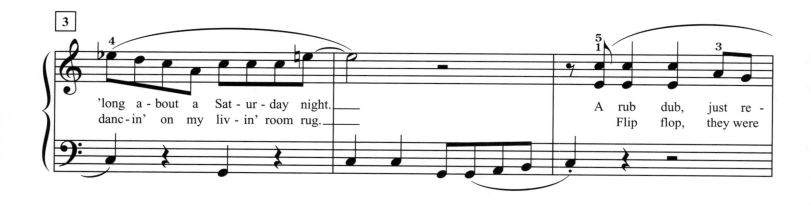

'long a - bout a Sat - ur - day night.___   A rub dub, just re -
danc - in' on my liv - in' room rug.___   Flip flop, they were

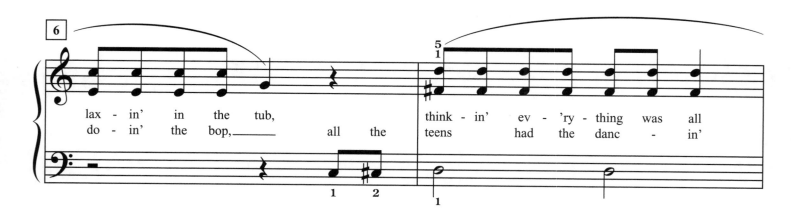

lax - in' in the tub,   think - in' ev - 'ry - thing was all
do - in' the bop,___ all the   teens had the danc - in'

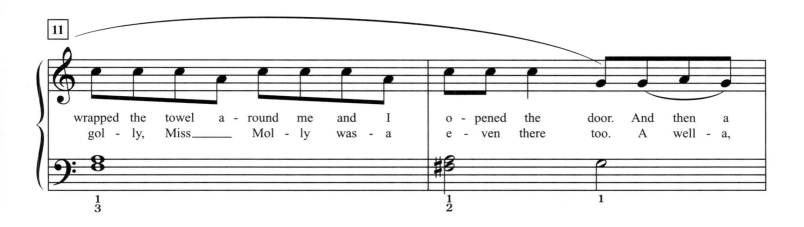

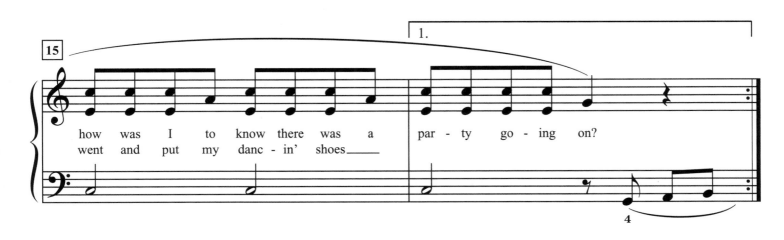

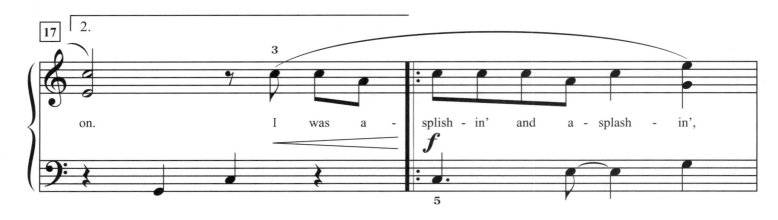

on.   I was a - splish - in' and a - splash - in',

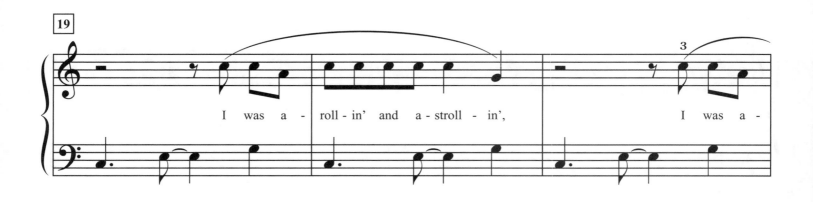

I was a - roll - in' and a - stroll - in',   I was a -

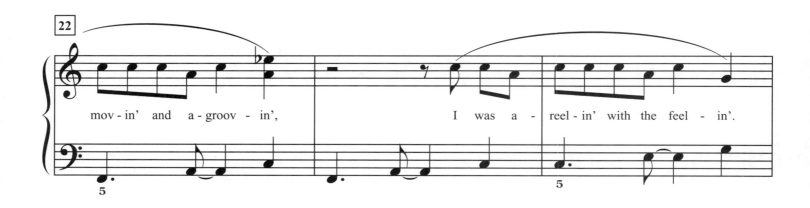

mov - in' and a - groov - in',   I was a - reel - in' with the feel - in'.

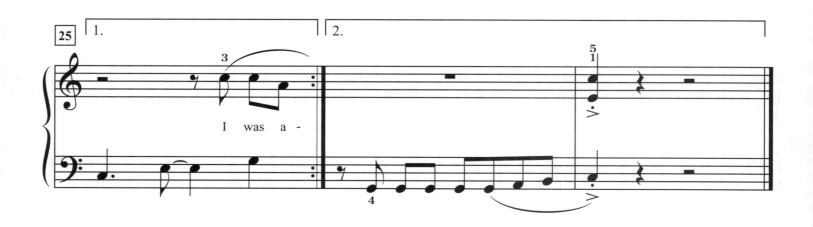

I was a -

A Teenager In Love

Words by Doc Pomus
Music by Mort Shuman
Arranged by Carol Matz

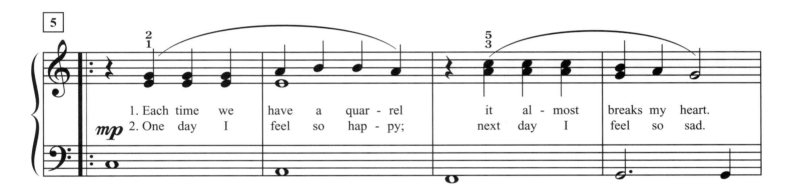

1. Each time we have a quar - rel it al - most breaks my heart.
2. One day I feel so hap - py; next day I feel so sad.

'Cause I am so a - fraid____ that we will have to part.)
I guess I'll learn to take____ the good with the bad.)

Each night I ask the stars up a - bove:

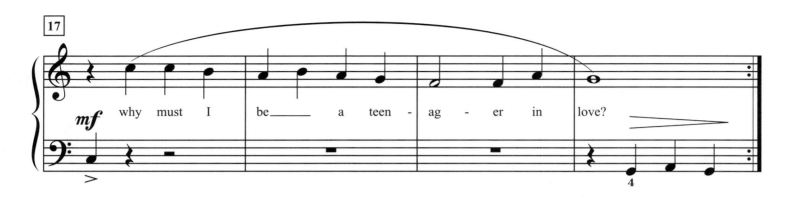

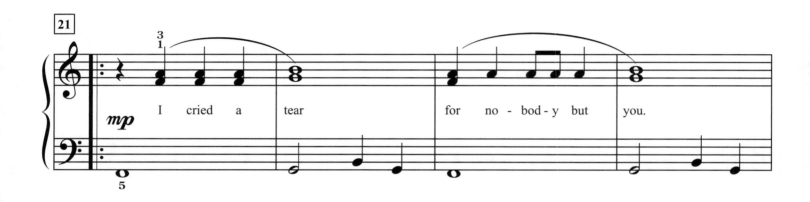

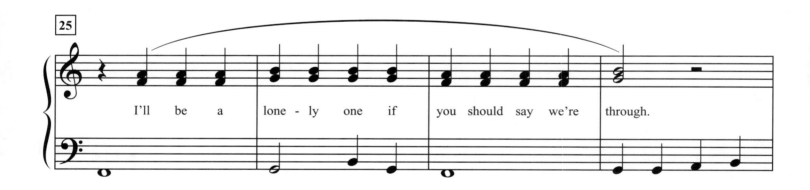

And if you should say good - bye,_____ I'll still go on lov - ing you.

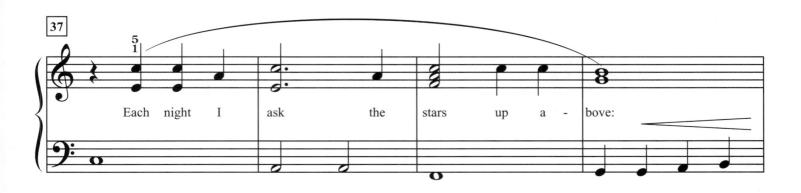

Each night I ask the stars up a - bove:

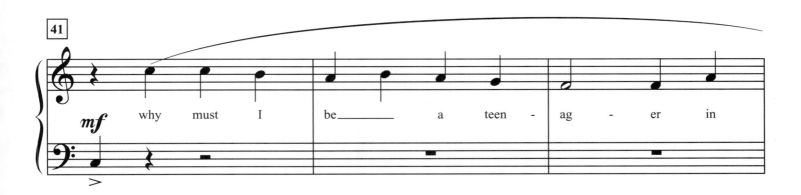

mf why must I be_____ a teen - ag - er in

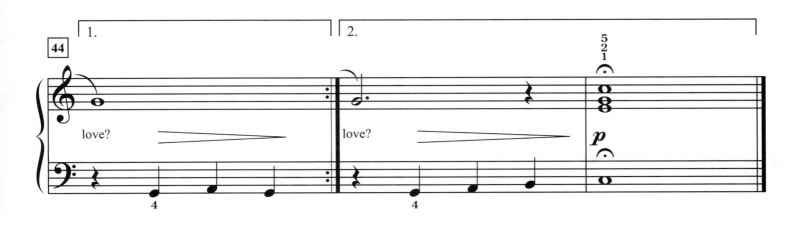

1. love? 2. love? *p*

That's Entertainment

Words by Howard Dietz
Music by Arthur Schwartz
Arranged by Carol Matz

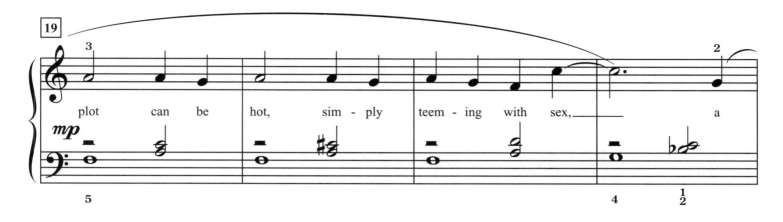

plot can be hot, sim - ply teem - ing with sex,_____ a

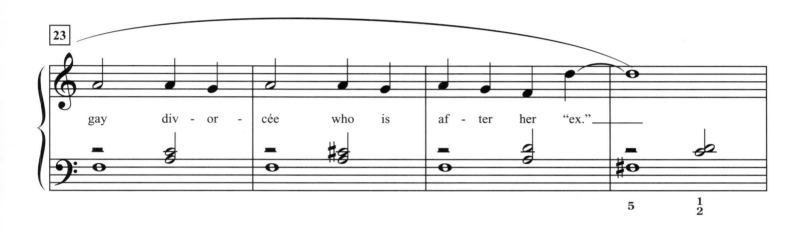

gay div - or - cée who is af - ter her "ex."_____

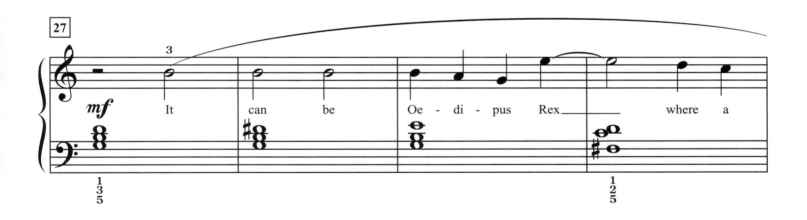

It can be Oe - di - pus Rex_____ where a

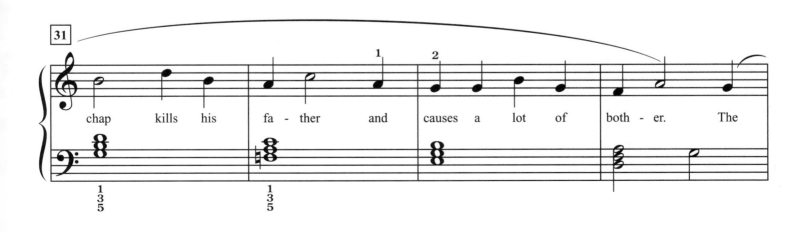

chap kills his fa - ther and causes a lot of both - er. The

Wipe Out

Words and Music by The Surfaris
Arranged by Carol Matz

74

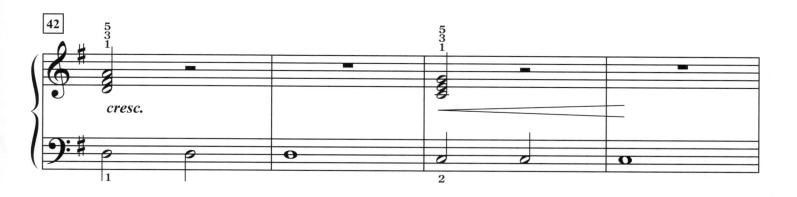

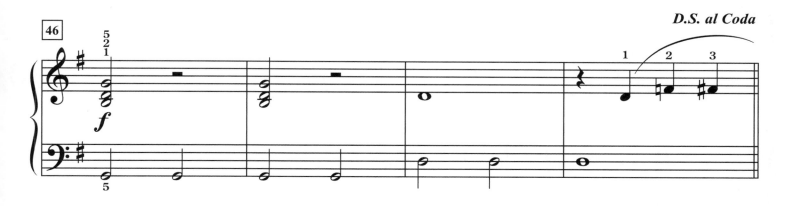

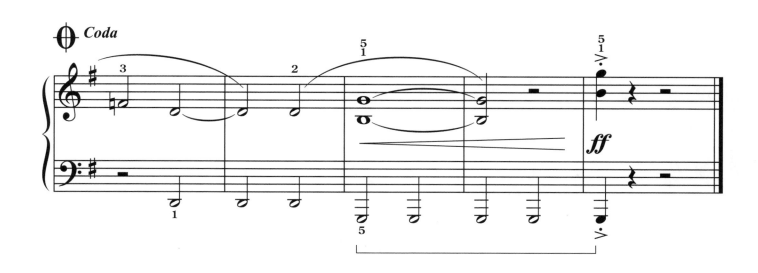

(We're Gonna) Rock Around the Clock

Words and Music by
Max C. Freedman and Jimmy DeKnight
Arranged by Carol Matz

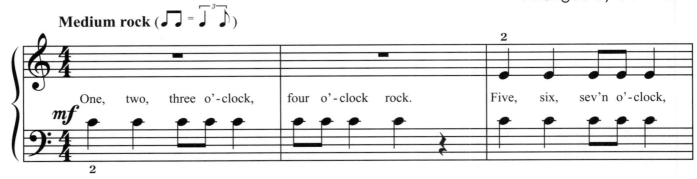

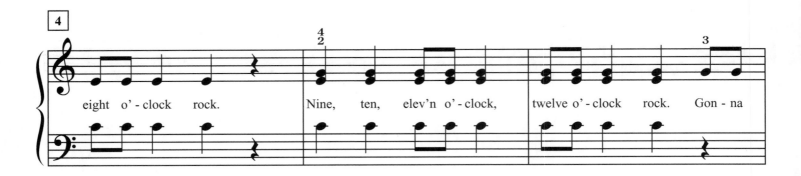

rock a - round the clock to - night,— gon - na rock, rock, rock 'til

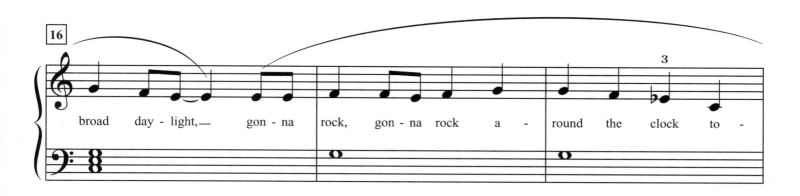

broad day - light,— gon - na rock, gon - na rock a - round the clock to -

night!—————— 2. When the clock strikes two and

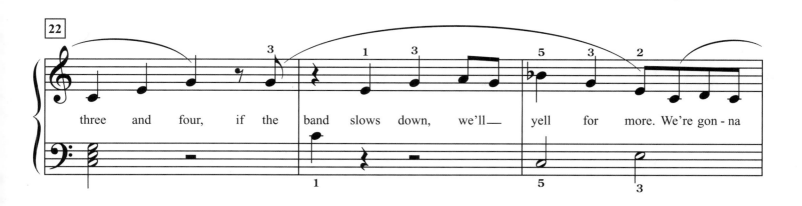

three and four, if the band slows down, we'll— yell for more. We're gon - na

rock a - round the clock to - night,— gon - na rock, rock, rock 'til

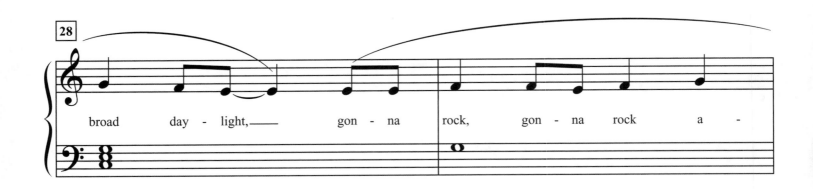

broad day - light,— gon - na rock, gon - na rock a -

round the clock to - night!

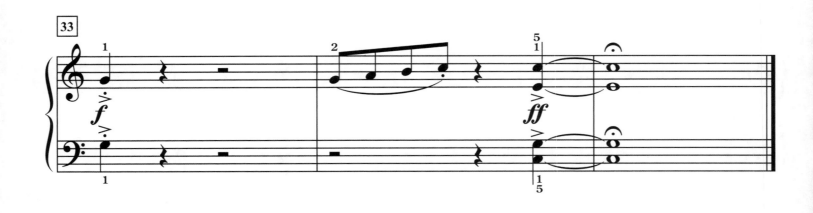